General Eisenhower

on the

Military Churchill

Edited by James Nelson

A Conversation with Alistair Cooke

With an Introduction by Alistair Cooke

General Eisenhower
on the
Military Churchill

W.W.Norton & Company.Inc.

New York

Contents

7 Editor's Note

9 With Eisenhower at Gettysburg
By Alistair Cooke

17 General Eisenhower on the Military Churchill

96 Acknowledgments

Editor's Note

The purpose of this conversation was to elicit from the Supreme Allied Commander, General Dwight D. Eisenhower, memories of his World War II comrade-in-arms, Winston Churchill. The aim was not a formal remembrance, but a personal memoir that would emanate spontaneously from informal talk.

Alistair Cooke was chosen as the person most exactly right to evoke such a memoir. He knew both Eisenhower and Churchill. Although born in England, he is now an American citizen, and chief American correspondent of the *Guardian* (of England). So his perspective on both men—and both countries—is unique. In addition, Mr. Cooke is well remembered by Americans as the amiable and sagacious host of the television series *Omnibus*.

To talk with General Eisenhower about the military Churchill, Alistair Cooke went to Gettysburg. It is not an easy place to reach. Mr. Cooke flew there by helicopter, just as Churchill did when he visited the General to bid him farewell. Mr. Cooke landed at the Eisenhower farm, next to the Gettysburg battlefield which Churchill had described as "a place revered by the manhood of the United States."

After the conversation was filmed for television, where it made its first appearance, a good deal of historically valuable information had to be sacrificed to accommodate the limits of television time. Now, fortunately, this material can be restored and exists in permanent form in this volume. Another feature of the book is the special introduction by Alistair Cooke, in which he writes of the General as he came to know him so informally during the several uninterrupted days in Gettysburg.

For the clarification of the reader, General Eisenhower and Alistair Cooke are identified by name at the beginning of their conversation. Thereafter, in order to avoid repeating the names, General Eisenhower's comments are in roman type and Mr. Cooke's words in italic.

JAMES NELSON

With Eisenhower at Gettysburg

By Alistair Cooke

Although as a working correspondent I had "covered" Eisenhower from the convention that nominated him on through his years as President, James Nelson's invitation to go to Gettysburg and spend some days talking with the General about Churchill was one I accepted with alacrity. During several years of moonlighting as a television master of ceremonies I had discovered that few casual experiences in peacetime offer such a rewarding and sustained glimpse

of a man as that of working alone with him on a long television dialogue.

Intelligent actors complain that the chronic ordeal of their profession is "the waiting, not the acting." But it is during the waiting intervals, which tend to be prolonged and uncertain, that you can sit down and talk usefully with a man to no set purpose. And during the three days at Gettysburg, I spent many hours alone with the General (as he preferred to be called) talking in his office, and up at the farm, about everything from politics to golf, from the code of a soldier to the temptations of a newspaperman, from the private trials of the Presidency to the public life of a small Kansas town in the early 1900s. We deliberately avoided elaborating on his reminiscences of Churchill, thinking it better to let these come out instinctively in the free-wheeling talk that was done under the cameras.

The General was always cordial and relaxed in the mornings and again at the end of day. In between, he was inclined to fret at the unsoldierly routine of waiting for action that was unscheduled and unpredictable, and very often he would glance at his watch and screw up his eyes— as he always did when in doubt or suspicion—and wonder "what those fellows are up to." Inevitably, I suppose, a lifelong officer is put at his ease by knowing precisely what his subordinates are doing and when they are expected to appear at the double. He could never understand why a change of lighting or camera set-up could take ten minutes or an hour, and to my assurances that everything was under control he would shake his head and concede that "it's a weird business." Then I would ask him about his favorite part of England, or what was the toughest course he had ever played, and he would light up again and be off in his earnest, restless, rollicking manner.

In the late afternoons, he retired to his house for a nap and soon afterwards appeared, amiable again. It was here that you could get an indelible impression of him in the years of his retirement. And it was here too that I found myself bringing into focus my own tentative judgment about his virtues in war and in peace.

10

By the time of this, our last, meeting, he was very much an old country squire, sitting on his terrace with his back to the light and the book held high in his hands because, like many old men whose eyesight does alarming things from month to month, he was just then in between prescriptions, so to speak. So his glasses were perched on the end of his nose, and by holding the book high and looking through the bottom of the lenses he could get things in focus until the new bifocals arrived. From time to time he put the book down and squinted out across his fields to the pasture. And he would watch the cattle going in, or scrutinize a blighted elm, or remark that a particular feed grass he was using burned out too quickly in the drenching summer heat of that very hot valley.

We all, they say, revert to our origins in old age, and if you'd not known who Ike was you would have guessed, and rightly, that he was a lifelong farmer—and by now a prosperous one. They were having a fierce drought that summer in Pennsylvania, as everywhere else in the East, and as the sun declined and the evening became bearable, we strolled out onto the grass and towards a small circular lawn that was a precious thing to Ike. It was a rudimentary putting green and it had only one hole, with a flag stuck in it whose pennant was stamped with the five stars of a General of the Army. But, strangely, this hole was invisible; it was so grown over with weeds that I doubt you could have sunk a small cannonball in it. I asked about this and he said, in that hesitant yet strenuous tone he brought to all questions of conscience: "Well, you see, the Governor of Pennsylvania put out a proclamation over a month ago, I guess, asking people to save water and do no watering of lawns, gardens, golf courses and so on. Looks pretty sad, doesn't it?"

In retrospect, it was altogether a sad occasion. In his old age, there were two things Ike lived for: his farm and his golf. And the greater of these was his golf. At that time he was beginning to be plagued by innumerable ailments, and I remember on that particular day he was a little querulous because he had had some tests made on

11

an affliction of his diaphragm, and the results were not in. But what worried him most was the arthritis in his hands. The next day he kept rubbing the joints and wondering if he would ever play golf again. I hinted, in a subsequent conversation, that he had the golf bug pretty badly. "In the worst way," he said. "I didn't really take it up until after the war when I was in my mid-fifties, when I was at SHAPE. And, as you know, it takes about two years to learn to hit the ball. And sometimes during briefing sessions, I'd let my mind wander from the disposition of the Russian armies and our NATO equipment and so on, and just worry about my game. There was a time when I used to dash out of Paris to St. Cloud and, by golly, I'd say never mind the Russian threat to Europe, if only I can straighten out this terrible duck-hook that I've developed."

If it happened just like that, I'm sure that no one felt more guilt about it than Ike. For he had, at all times, an overwhelming sense of mission—whether you agreed or not with the mission didn't matter. While he was in Paris, and while he was in the Presidency, there were certain priorities in his mind that had the force of moral absolutes. One was the security of Western Europe, and we ought not to forget, in the ups and downs of European independence, that it was Ike's authority, and the certainty of the attitude he conveyed to the Russians, which kept Europe untouched in the dangerous days when the Soviet Union was sorely tempted to move into the southern periphery of Europe. It is a curious psychological fact, never satisfactorily explained, why the Russians seemed to respect the peaceful intentions of a professional soldier more than they did those of Ike's predecessor or his successors. Although American presidential election campaigns tend, by their ferocity and length, to cause the parties to over-dramatize their differences and pretend they are offering the people drastically opposite policies, it may appear in time that American foreign policy, towards Europe anyway, was all of a piece from the day that President Truman warned the Russians about Greece to the day that President Johnson warned them again about Berlin. But the man who secured this policy and gave it stamina was

Eisenhower. And for that, perhaps more than anything else, I believe, we are all in his debt.

Whether he was a great President, or even a very good one, is something that I don't think it possible to decide today. Arnold Toynbee, for example, has the rather alarming conviction that the man responsible for our present ills and the coming of Doomsday is Truman, and that John Foster Dulles's brinkmanship was only a way of saying what Truman had long ago been doing. Eisenhower, it seems to me, had two golden periods, of which the second was his first term as President. The first, of course, began with his appointment as Supreme Commander of the Allied Forces.

Many harsh things have been said about him as a soldier and about the "luck" of his promotion, over many superiors, to the American command in Europe. Among European commentators, Eisenhower's total inexperience as a field commander is by now almost a byword. From this literal fact the false inference is readily drawn that he was essentially a desk man quite out of touch with the demands of modern war. Nothing could be farther from the truth or, incidentally, reflect so poorly on General Marshall's judgment. Marshall had watched Eisenhower's masterly conduct of the vast Louisiana maneuvers in September 1941, a field exercise involving a quarter of a million men in a "war" of supply that few old field commanders had ever experienced.

It is true that Ike's most recent professional experience, that of creating a defense for the Philippines, brought him into immediate close contact with Marshall in the days after Pearl Harbor when the Philippines were the most vulnerable of America's outposts in the Pacific. But a desk man would have been routinely consulted and dismissed. Marshall threw at Ike the whole strategical problem of the Pacific, and Ike's quick decision that Australia must become the essential base to build and hold for the protection of China, the Philippines, and the Dutch East Indies coincided with Marshall's private, and unexpressed, judgment. Moreover, Marshall had at his elbow innumerable Eisenhower reports on what the shape of a two-ocean war might be. For, during his years as confidential adviser to the Army Chief of Staff, Eisenhower had become absorbed by the probable scope and character of a future global war: by "such subjects as the mobilization and composition of armies, the role of air forces and navies in war, tending toward mechanization, and the acute dependence of all elements of military life upon the industrial capacity of the nation. This last was to me of especial importance because of my intense belief that large-scale motorization and mechanization and the development of air forces in unprecedented strength would characterize successful military forces of the future." * These were subjects that too many distinguished veterans of the First World War, among both the British and the French, were only too ready to dismiss in the 1930s as Wellsian fantasies. At any rate, once Marshall had successfully resisted Roosevelt's persistent pleas to take the Supreme Command himself, no other candidate than Eisenhower was considered.

Eisenhower may not have been, like Montgomery or Rommel, a soldier's soldier (which, for good or ill, means a practiced old warrior). But he was, for the war years, the ideal choice for a human task which the Allies of the First World War, bristling with a long tradition of military chauvinism, so stubbornly and grievously evaded: that of uniting by his own likeable and fair personality the warring elements of many allied nations, many diverse temperaments, and some very rum characters. The one touch of genius he had was that of a peacemaker among Americans, Englishmen, Frenchmen, Poles, and others bristling with national pride and driven by ambition. It may be, indeed, that such immortality as Eisenhower achieves will be guaranteed by two qualities that do not usually, in a worldly world, secure a man much more than the affection of his friends. By the force of these qualities, Eisenhower was able to make trusting friends of about 250 million people fighting for their lives. They are candor and decency.

* *Crusade In Europe,* p. 19.

14

General Eisenhower

on the

Military Churchill

ALISTAIR COOKE: *General Eisenhower, you were the American, who, I suppose, saw more of Churchill during the Second World War, saw more of him on crucial occasions, than anyone else. And I was fascinated that when he died, and you came to pay tribute to him on the BBC, you hailed him as soldier, citizen, statesman. And you put the word "soldier" first.*

GENERAL EISENHOWER: Deliberately. I met Mr. Churchill right after America entered the war. And I found at once that his dedication to victory was so complete, his interest in every facet of the war— strategic, tactical, logistic—was so great that he practically made himself a member of the British Chiefs of Staff.

As such did he conduct himself as an equal?

Once Mr. Churchill said in a meeting: "All I want is compliance with my wishes, after reasonable discussion."

17

General, how did he conduct—if it was his job to conduct—a military meeting?

He would sit down and say, "Now gentlemen, we have this proposition." And he would bring it out himself, not having a secretary. Then he would invite discussion on a topic, usually selecting the officer most concerned.

When the thing was over, if it called for any immediate decision, he might make some recommendation. Usually, it was just for everybody's information. But he did it all in a very informal way. There was no punctilio.

And he didn't lecture and lecture?

No, although I'll say this: when he got into a discussion about anything, he never just commented. He would give a little bit of an oration. It might be short, but still you felt like it was an oration. Sometimes it almost silenced you. And he could use anything. He used pathos. I've seen tears run over his chin, you know, right down from his eyes when he'd talk. One night, there was something that he wanted to do in Italy; and I was telling him the impossibility. And he painted a terrible picture if we didn't do it. I'll never forget the terms he used. He said, "If that should happen I should have to go to His Majesty and lay down the mantle of my high office." And here were tears running down. But within ten seconds he was telling a joke.

The man could use pathos, humor, anecdote, history, anything to get his own way. And, as I say, he dearly loved to have his own way. And always remember this, ninety percent of all the meetings ended amicably and profitably for everybody. Everybody had better understanding, and better co-ordination had been achieved.

Eisenhower demonstrates Churchill's use of pathos at a military meeting. "Tears were running down his cheeks. But within ten seconds he was telling a joke."

Some junior—relatively junior—officer told me that they had to be very careful when they were reporting casualties to Churchill.

I remember one night we were down at Checquers at a late conference. And there was a logistic presentation about the amount of free shipping space. We had to reinforce certain elements. There was this fellow doing a very good job of reporting. Finally, he used the phrase "so many thousand bodies." Mr. Churchill broke in with great indignation and said, "Sir, you will not refer to the personnel of His Majesty's Forces in any such term as 'bodies.' They're not corpses. They are live men, that's what they are. I want to hear no more of the word."

19

Were you surprised at his depth or width of knowledge of actual military matters? Did he not have it as far as tactics are concerned?

Yes, he did. I think when you get down to minor tactics you'd have to exclude that. But the general rules, you might say the basic rules—a lack of dispersion, and using your mass, using surprise—all that kind of thing—he knew instinctively.

You know that he was at the bottom of his class at Harrow, a total flop at school. But then when he went to Sandhurst he was head of his class in tactics and fortifications. Is that a regular course at West Point, fortifications?

Yes. When I was at West Point we were still talking about the Bourbon fortresses the Frenchmen designed for all of Europe. Of course, it is the business of West Point to teach basics. I've often repeated to young

Churchill maintained close association with the troops. On an inspection tour he gestures with knife used by commandos.

21

officers what I learned from a Staff Instructor at West Point. He said: "Everything changes in war—weapons, logistics, terrain. But *never* human nature. Alexander the Great's men suffered the same emotional fears and doubts as are endured today. A student of modern warfare will be wise to keep all of that in mind."

By the way, this thing about Churchill being at the top of his class: at the risk of being a little bit immodest, I want to tell you that in West Point I had a very mediocre record. In discipline, for example, I think I was 125 out of 162. But when I went, five or ten years later, to Leavenworth, which was a very tough competitive school in those days, I was number one in the class. So you can't tell when people begin to mature. In any event, there's a parallel. That's the reason I mentioned something that sounds otherwise very immodest. The parallel is between his rather mediocre academic record and when he got a profession to think about. Then he did better.

To be blunt, you sort of came from the ranks to become the Supreme Allied Commander. Did you ever expect at the beginning of '41, for instance, to win the war with Churchill?

Not at all. As a matter of fact, I wasn't even made a temporary Colonel until March of '41. Then, when we got into the various areas of training and maneuvers in this country, I finally was put up one grade to temporary Brigadier General.

Was that as a result of your part in the Louisiana maneuvers?

Apparently.

22

Which was when, January?

No, it was in September of '41. That was when, in a time of national peril, our Congress by only one vote kept the draft act in our laws; and that margin only through the efforts of General Marshall. I was brought into the War Department itself, I suppose, partially because of recommendations by friends to the Chiefs of Staff. But largely, also, because I'd had so much service in the Philippines and they, for the moment, were engaging all our time and attention. Then as I got to working in the Staff, I was responsible for drawing up the original "Roundup" which became the "Overlord" plan.

Which was the invasion of France?

That's right. When it reached General Marshall, he approved it and took it to the President. The President sent Marshall over to get Mr. Churchill's approval. It was all done. From that time on "Overlord" became the guiding principle—no matter what else took place, it became the guide for everything we did in Europe. I'd drawn up this plan and believed in it. Not many did in our Army, I tell you. I think General Marshall decided that since I'd drawn it up I ought to be sent over there. That's where my intimate acquaintance with the Prime Minister began. I guess it was early June 1942, although I had met him briefly in December.

He and I seemed to get along at ease and with understanding. I must say that not only did I have a great affection for the man but my admiration for him in conference, for his keen mind, and of course for his ability to express himself—all of these impressed me wonderfully.

23

Can you throw your mind back, General, to the first time you met him on a professional basis as soldier to soldier, when you had to get down to tactics and strategy?

Well, the very first time I came over I was not the commander. General Marshall sent me over to see what our own group of Americans in London were doing. They were called American observers. As a matter of fact, even after we'd gotten into the war they were wearing civilian clothes weekends.

The relationship between the two leaders was one of comradeship and understanding.

But they were professional soldiers.

Yes. But they were called observers. So he sent me over to see what was going on. And I met and had a long and serious conversation with the Prime Minister in London at that time. Told him what we hoped to do. If you will recall, the British and Americans had worked out, before we were in the war, what was called the ABC plan. It was a plan that said that if we were to get into a war as allies, in two oceans, we would first attack the European end of the Axis. Destroying that, we'd go on to take care of the Pacific. Well, when I talked to him first, he had been party to that operation. So from there we began to talk about the ways of getting into Europe and doing our part in bringing Hitler to his knees. That always was the basis of our conversations. Mr. Churchill was intensely interested in all warfare, going way back. He would talk about the battle of Cannae just as well as could a professional soldier. And he'd written that magnificent biography of his warrior ancestor—Marlborough.

Churchill was so interested in every detail, he would frequently send telegrams to soldiers in the field and want to know about a particular regiment or brigade or division and what it was doing, and so on. General Marshall never asked a thing like that in the whole time I was in the field.

Did you ever suggest to Churchill, or did it occur to him, how a Field Commander might feel if he gets one of these knuckle-rapping telegrams?

Well, he wanted the Battle of Alamein to start in September rather than October. The plan of General Alexander was to have it go on the October moon, they call it. And he sent for me one day and said,

26

"Here's a cable I'm sending to General Alexander."

I thought it was really questioning Alexander's judgment, and I said, "Well, Prime Minister, if that had come to me from my American Commanders I would have to resign." He was so completely startled he said, "What do you mean?"

And I said, "Well, this looks as though you, who are three thousand miles away," or whatever it was—fifteen hundred miles—"that you feel that you are more competent to judge on the readiness of this army to attack, its morale, its equipment, its strength, its positions, training, and everything, than is General Alexander. This I don't think is possible."

He said, "As a military man and as the Chief Minister of His Majesty, don't I have the right to ask questions?"

I said, "I think you have the right to ask questions, but it ought to be done to show real respect for this man's ability."

So he said, "I think maybe you're right. I will put it really in the form of a query."

And I said, "I think that's perfectly logical."

Yes, I must say it must be pretty tough to be a Field Commander and feel that you own the universe that you can see, and then get the kind of order which was Churchill's order to Alexander in Cairo, "Your prime and main duty will be to take and destroy at the earliest opportunity the German-Italian Army commanded by Field Marshal Rommel, together with all its supplies and establishment in Egypt and Libya."

Well, he didn't leave anything out. But Alexander's reply some months later surely delighted Churchill. Alexander cabled: "Sir, your orders to me of August 15, 1942, have been fulfilled. I now await your further orders."

Churchill could be rather trenchant, if not a little bit sarcastic, you know, in giving orders. One he sent to the C & O, usually called the First Sea Lord. Its general sense was: "I have received your message. May I remind you that warships are meant to go under fire. Churchill."

And to the Chief Marshal for Air he said, "I'm glad you have the matter, as you say, under examination. Pray report to me tomorrow what is going to be done. Churchill."

That doesn't give much room to quarrel, does it?

Of course, I suppose that he was such a tremendous moral figure in Britain, especially during the dark days, that everybody had to put up with this.

May, 1941. Churchill stands among the rubble in Parliament's bombed-out debating chamber.

As a matter of fact, I don't think they felt that there was anything wrong. This was his method. And he so personified Britain at that moment that I think everybody expected it. The only man I ever heard complain a little bit about it was General Brooke. He was a very sensitive person. And what he complained most about was the hours that the Prime Minister would keep him up to discuss the tactics and strategy of the war. After about two o'clock, Brookey would get pretty tired.

You know, Roosevelt had the same problem because there was a good deal of sporting jealousy between them in the ability to tell stories. Roosevelt fancied himself a great storyteller. I remember when we went up to Quebec on the train. Churchill didn't get going till about eleven P.M., and Roosevelt was doing his damnedest to keep up with him, and finally collapsed. They took him away; and Churchill ordered up some refreshments. They brought him a glass of milk. He threw it out, you know. He said, "This is for babies. It's three A.M., and I want refreshment."

General, when you first arrived in Britain before you were Supreme Commander, did you notice any difference in the tradition of running a war? I'm thinking about the chain of command, as between the United States and Britain.

It was quite a difference. And each of us had to make concessions. For example, they would have three commanders-in-chief: a commander in ground, air, and sea. These people would get together and make the different plans for coordination, action, and battles. Now with us in the United States, it's a very simple thing. The War Department and the government decide that they have to do a certain thing with military forces. They look at the problem and say,

"This is the mission for our forces." They pick a man. They confer with him about how much he'll need: how many divisions, how much air and navy, and all the rest of it. Then they say, all right, it's *your* job.

From then on it's his responsibility. He stays in command if he's successful; he's taken out if he's a failure. If you read the story of our Civil War it's just a quick rotation of single high commanders right along through to the Potomac.

Well, didn't Lincoln say, "When the man is in the field he's the boss?"

That's right. That is correct. Anyway, with give and take here and there and making allowances for Mr. Churchill's participation, I became the Supreme Allied Commander in the west. Now I must say this: Churchill did accept our idea that in the field there must be one commander in any one theater of war. That was a very great concession, because the British didn't really believe in it. I think the generals finally came to believe that it was good. But it was very hard for them to accept that originally.

But wouldn't this make you, as the Supreme Commander, the arbiter between any competing authority or ambition between two field commanders? I mean, for instance, between two armies?

Yes.

And you were given total freedom?

I was given total freedom. At one time General Brooke, Chief of the Imperial General Staff, accompanied by the Prime Minister, came down on a special trip to see me and said, "Now look, General, we know that with the American forces you've got absolute authority—you can demote and send home, you can do anything, you can promote, and every man here is your choice."

I said, "That's correct."

He said, "We want you to know you have that same authority with us. If there's anybody from the highest to the lowest you don't want, you let us know and he'll be removed."

General, in the long year between Pearl Harbor and the invasion of Africa, I know that Churchill was greatly troubled by the fact that the Russians were wondering if we were ever going to help them in Europe, because they were in mortal danger. What was the strategy which led up to the choice of Africa as the point to invade?

Well, it is true that both governments, the United States and British, had agreed that there must be some ground action in the eastern Atlantic, or that general theater of war, so as to encourage not only the Russians but ourselves. One of them was an attack on Norway, and that looked rather barren and unpromising and seemed to be off center. Another was the possibility of going across the Channel and capturing the port of Cherbourg and part of the peninsula below that. We hoped to hold that as a sort of a fortress, right on the mainland, and be a threat to the German forces.

A third possibility was to go into Northwest Africa —an operation called Torch—and to help the British coming from Cairo to destroy the Axis in Africa. So it came down to a debate between the Cross-Channel effort to seize a bridgehead, and Torch. Without detailing all of the reasons, for a while the Americans stood for the Cross-Channel seizure of a bridgehead; and Mr. Churchill and his staff, for Torch—North

Invasion points considered for a first landing by U.S. and
British troops: Norway, Cherbourg, and Northwest Africa.

Africa. The debate continued until Churchill advised
us that Torch would not delay the eventual invasion of
Europe.

With this assurance, General Marshall said, "Well,
here we go." And the Torch plan was undertaken. In
after months I became absolutely certain that Mr.
Churchill had been right in his argument for that particular operation; and so did General Marshall.

FOLLOWING PAGES An Allied Planning Conference, Algiers, 1943. Prime Minister
Winston Churchill (center) with (left to right), Rt. Hon.
Anthony Eden; General Alan Brooke; Air Chief Marshal
Arthur W. Tedder; Admiral Sir Andrew Cunningham; General
Harold R.L.G. Alexander; General George C. Marshall;
General Dwight D. Eisenhower; and General Sir Bernard L.
Montgomery.

North Africa. Churchill's hat raised in anticipation of
triumph to come.

General, talking about who had authority over whom, it strikes me it must have been a pleasure to you to be able to, at certain times, exercise your own authority over Churchill. I'm thinking that he wanted to go, didn't he, with the first wave into Normandy? And you had to stop him?

That's correct. He came and said that he expected to go, and I said, "I don't think you should." I said, "Frankly, I can't go on the first wave for the simple reason I have to be at the center of communications. But I think that you are just too valuable to the whole Allied cause, and I don't believe you should run the risk of running into a mine."

What did he say to that?

He said, "I think that the First Minister of His Majesty ought to be along to see an event such as this, and I think I should go." I said, "Well, I'll tell you this, you'll never do it with my consent." And he thought a second—he was very sharp, you know— and he said, "General, as I understand, your authority is absolute as far as the operation Overlord is concerned, and this operation of D-Day."

"Yes, that is correct."

"And therefore you can allow such visitors as you want."

"Yes."

He said, "But you have no authority whatsoever on the administrative side of His Majesty's forces."

"No, I don't."

"Then of course I can ship along in one of the ships as a member of the crew and you can do nothing about it."

"No," I said, "I can't do anything about it, except that I'd worry. And I think it's rather unfair to give me another burden on a day like this."

Churchill was determined to join the first wave of troops into
Normandy on D-Day. King George VI became involved. Here
the two men stand together on the balcony of Buckingham
Palace, V-E Day, May 8, 1945.

39

That ended it. I didn't know what he was going to do. But a little later I heard that word of this came to the King, George VI. So he sent a message to the Prime Minister and praised the Prime Minister and said, "And because you're going, of course I'm going along, too, because it's not fitting that you should go along at the head of my troops unless I'm there." And this stopped it. There was no more said about it.

You know, somewhere Churchill defines democracy as "the occasional necessity of deferring to the opinions of others." I think this is a definition that must have had great meaning for him when you came to the conflict about going up through the south of France. As I understand it, when D-Day was successful the plan had been agreed on, an all-out plan to break from the Mediterranean up through the south of France. Churchill was suddenly overcome with this great desire to go up through Austria—to send Alexander through Austria. Would you tell us about that, General?

The real thing was, were we going to win the war just as fast as we could with one great big powerful blow, with the aid of a secondary attack from the south? Or were we going to delay the completion of the war for other purposes?

I strongly believed that the Allied Armies, moving out from the D-Day beaches, should be supported by an army to come up from the Mediterranean. And that such a southern port should be open to us for later troop arrivals from the States. This military action was approved by all the Allies at the highest levels. The troops for Anvil-Dragoon—the code name for the attack from the south of France—were to be withdrawn from Italy. Of course, that meant slowing our northern advance in that country.

40

As you say, Churchill became attracted by the idea of keeping intact the forces in Italy and fighting up into Austria—as far as Vienna; that was his hope. So, D-Day happened. After it, we finally broke out of the bridgehead about August first. We were then sweeping across France on our right flank and were

Eisenhower urged the Anvil-Dragoon attack from the south of France to support forces in Normany invading from the beaches. Troops for Anvil-Dragoon would be withdrawn from Italy, a plan Churchill opposed. He had wanted those forces to attack up through Austria.

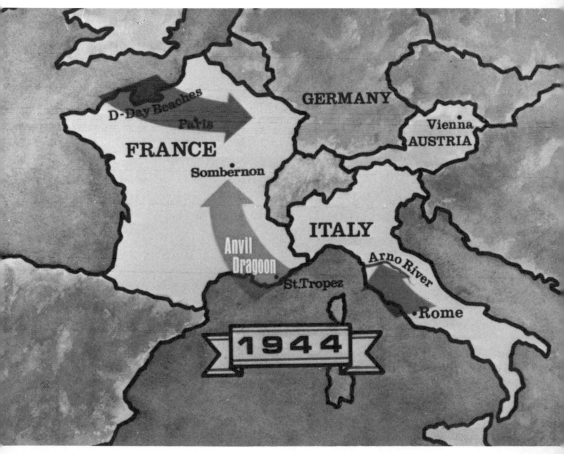

involved in the great battle of Falaise, which many people said was the greatest killing ground of the war. Unfortunately too many people escaped from the killing—our enemies. But this success put into the Prime Minister's mind the conviction that we no longer needed the attack in the south and that we should leave all of those troops with Alexander and let him go on up through the Ljubljana Gap into Austria. He argued that wholly on military grounds. It was a *seven-hour argument* one afternoon.

With Churchill?

Yes, in my headquarters. Churchill had with him my great friend, Admiral Sir Andrew Cunningham, who believed as his Prime Minister did. But my directive from the Joint Chiefs of Staff, Combined Chiefs of Staff, was very clear: "You will proceed toward the heart of Germany and destroy Hitler's armed forces." It said nothing other than that. So I told the Prime Minister if he wanted to cancel the southern supporting action in order to have a better positioning of the Allied forces at the end of the war, I'd understand because I knew that wars are waged for political purposes. "But," I said, "if you do that you must go to the President and get his agreement to change my orders. If he does, I'll go along.*

"But," I said, "if you're talking about the quickest way to destroy Hitler, we must adhere to our original plan." Because we—the Americans—had lost our artificial harbor, up there on the western beach. Cherbourg had proved to be a very unsatisfactory port, because the railway lines coming out of there were so tortuous and long that we'd pile up more supplies than we could bring out of the place. And Brest was just no good. We knew that when the Germans surrendered Brest the port was going to take a year to restore because they really were doing a job of destruction.

And so we needed Marseilles down there in the south. Besides, it was closer to our right flank down in the Metz area than was Cherbourg. Also, the Mediterranean and the south were just the easiest way to supply and bring in more troops from America. You see, we had finally got sixty-three American divisions into Europe, and we wanted to hit a sledge-hammer blow.

Now Mr. Churchill argued that we didn't need that. We had them licked already. I said, "Oh, no, we haven't." In later years, Churchill said that what was in his mind was to neutralize Soviet influence in that region. But at the time, he based his arguments solely on military considerations.

I know it was a deep disappointment to him that he couldn't have his Balkan Plan accepted. But did he accept the decision with good grace when it came?

Oh, indeed! The original name for the attack up from the South of France was Anvil. But it was changed to Dragoon. And he said that was very apt because he was dragooned into it. Not only that, but he immediately flew off to the Mediterranean and got in one of the destroyers that was going in on the landing. He was part of the bombarding team, for all I know. But he was out there right on the front lines, on the front sea lines, looking at the thing.

* Editor's note:
Churchill showed Eisenhower a protesting cable he had sent to President Roosevelt. The next day the reply came. The President said that after consulting with his Chiefs of Staff, he strongly supported Dragoon as of "great assistance to Eisenhower in driving the Huns from France."

Churchill observing the Dragoon landing.

He did go to lots of places, didn't he, I mean on all the fronts?

Well, for example, I told him he shouldn't go across the Rhine on the day of the twenty-fourth. (Of course, that crossing by Montgomery up north of the Ruhr was the third one of our troops getting across.) But the situation still was what we called a power thing; and we expected a great deal of reaction, particularly artillery shelling. There was nothing, very little reaction. So, during the morning—that was along about ten o'clock or something like that—I had to leave.

Where were you now?

I was right up there with him. We were up in a tower, overlooking the Rhine.

Incidentally, that's when he said—he and Brooke together said—"Thank God, General, you stood by your plans." He said, "The man is licked, we've got him. If he's got any sense he'll surrender right now." Oh, they were very, very jubilant that morning. So I started off. I had to go see General Bradley, a little further south. And I thought I had Churchill's promise not to go over. I hadn't been gone five minutes and he was right in a boat and going across. He had a great joy just putting his foot on the other side of the Rhine. I had already been over myself—down at Remagen I'd gone over. But I wasn't as important to the cause as that fellow was.

You said that he said "you're right," and they were licked.

Yes.

46

He had a great joy just putting his foot on the other side of
the Rhine.

Of course they weren't licked?

They were, yes. The reason they were licked was because at the same time that Montgomery got over here we were shooting out from the Remagen bridgehead joining up with Patton down to Frankfurt—joining up with Patton in a great encircling movement. A great double encirclement. Here was Field Marshal Walther von Model with a great army of three hundred and fifty to four hundred thousand German troops in the Ruhr. Now we had surrounded him. And as you saw that movement developing, and he couldn't get out, you knew that the war was—in a military sense—over. But Hitler held on because he said he was going to bring down Germany with him. And he almost did.

Of course they weren't licked?

They *were* licked, yes.

Eisenhower graphically describes the great double
encirclement surrounding Field Marshal von Model's armies.

Captured German officers.

General, looking back on it, somebody said that any man who had been in command in two wars always tried to fight the first one. What occurs to me is that the southern France adventure Churchill had in mind —and his later desire to get in through the Balkans and up to Berlin—was fighting Gallipoli over again; to knock the Turks out and to take the strain from the East. And also, of course, as a Briton, to assure control after the war of the Middle East, which was a fetish with British statesmen.

50

I one time jokingly asked the Prime Minister, "Now you're not trying to get over into the Balkans just to prove that you were right in World War I? Look, I'll admit that the Gallipoli concept was a brilliant one in view of the conditions in France at that time. And only bad management elsewhere defeated your objective. But we're fighting another war, not that one."

He just laughed at me and said, "You know better than that." The fact is that many people think he just liked that phrase, "The soft underbelly." Well, I don't see anything soft about the Alp Mountains, I'll tell you that.

We know that Churchill was very punctilious about protocol. Is it true, General, that he always put you on his right at dinner?

That's correct. And even when my rank was one full grade below that of others, he did it on the theory that anybody who held a commission from two nations always outranked anybody that had a commission from one. So I can't recall a single time, except once, when he didn't put me on his right. And then he called me up—I didn't realize he was quite so punctilious—he called me up and he said, "My old friend Field Marshal Smuts is to dinner with us this evening. Won't you give up your place on my right and take a place on my left?" I happened to be trying to be facetious and said, "Why Prime Minister, put me on the seat closest to the kitchen. I have an enormous appetite and I will get fed very well there." But he was very serious about it. He said, "My dear General, you will be near and on my left. I ask it only for one night."

And Churchill had once been Smuts' prisoner in the Boer War?

Yes, that's right.

I must say, General, it was something of a disability to have a tremendous appetite in Britain in wartime. Did they satisfy it in any special way?

Yes. As a matter of fact, we always had nice lunches. I had lunch with the Prime Minister every Tuesday normally, just the two of us. And one day he had an Irish stew prepared in a different way. Instead of having

Eisenhower and Churchill often lunched together in London.
Here the two men converse after lunch.

the usual amount of gravy and sauce which we have around ours it had a cover, you know, a pie crust over it. But because of food shortages in England, it was long on potatoes. However, it had a fair amount of meat; the sauce and crust were delicious. I said so. The Prime Minister said, "After this, it will be our main dish for Tuesday lunches." It was. And I enjoyed it. He always had something in all of his dinners, or lunches, that was a little bit different. I remember once he had found some eggs, plover eggs. They were golden plover, and I think it was illegal to have them. But he had a couple brought in. It was the first time I'd ever tasted them. I loved them. He was so very proud of them. He was always finding some special thing.

Did you ever feel, General, that because of his good relationship with you and because you were so physically close, that if he didn't get something out of President Roosevelt he might try it out on you?

Well, he might have done it . . . put it on the basis of a military thing. If I thought he was right militarily, of course I could change. But suppose I tried to do something on a political basis? I said to him, "You'd fire me, and you should." A soldier is not supposed to do this.

I reminded him that once he gave me a darn good scolding because down in the Mediterranean, in order to have a few days to move our field forces and our planes over to Italy and get in closer, I had to stop bombing for about five days to be able to pick up the steel plates, bombs, and such. So I tried to make a virtue of necessity. I published a little proclamation, put it on the radio. I said I was stopping bombing for five or six days just to give the Italian people a chance to see how nice it would be to get away from bombing and to make peace and surrender. Well, he sent a cable to Mr. Roosevelt and said, "Why are these soldiers getting into our political business? They're supposed to fight." So I had to explain the whole thing, and he took it with good grace.

Of course this whole approach—the Balkans or annihilating the German army—built into the big dispute which I suppose will be argued until the end of time, about the occupation of Berlin. Will you tell us about that General?

Well, my plan never did make Berlin itself an objective. So far as I was concerned, it was to destroy the armed forces of the enemy. And all my training in war is that geographical objectives are not the proper objectives. The enemy is. That is what you go after.

My own feeling was this: Political decisions had already divided Germany for occupational purposes. Remember that. There was no possibility of the Western Allies capturing Berlin and staying there. If we'd captured it, the agreements were made and approved. And, in fact, after the fighting stopped, we had to retreat from Leipzig 125 miles to get back into our own zone.

Now, this brings up two things. One, was it tactically possible, under the situation we then had, to capture Berlin? And, second, what did we hope to gain? Because, as I said, we had to retreat back to our own place as quickly as the fighting was over. Just remember this, when my final plans were issued, we were about two hundred miles to the westward of Berlin. The Russians, ready to attack, were thirty miles off Berlin, eastward, but with a bridgehead already west of the Oder River. It didn't seem to be good sense to try, both of us, to throw in forces toward Berlin and get mixed up—two armies that couldn't talk the same language, couldn't even communicate with each other.

55

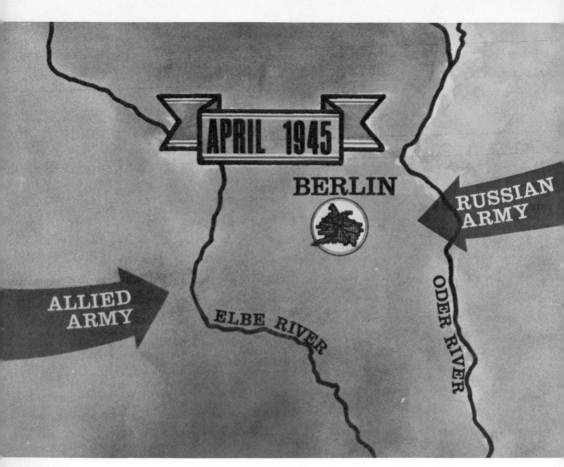

Allied and Russian Army positions, April 1945.

It would have been a terrible mess. What would be the gain? Today people have said, well, we'd have gotten prestige. I just want to know whether this matter of prestige was worth, let's say, ten thousand American and British lives, and possibly thirty thousand.

General Bradley put it much higher, didn't he?

He put it much higher. But I say, just take that. What was this prestige we were supposed to get? We'd won the war and we'd gone much further than our own political bosses apparently thought we could and argued we could. So I think this argument of Monday-morning quarterbacks is a little bit silly.

Now remember, Mr. Churchill always talked about this campaign, before we launched it, as requiring something on the order of two years. In eleven months it was all done and ended. Why suddenly the belief that everything was a blunder? You'd think that we'd lost the war. I don't think we did.

General, one thing occurs to me. There's a voice in this whole argument—this apparently perennial argument —that has never been heard, since General Marshall refused to write his memoirs. But we now find that he did tape forty-five hours, and he left it, and it's all in the George C. Marshall Library in Lexington, Virginia. It so happens that we have a tape of his opinion about the capture of Berlin. Do you think we should listen to it?

General George C. Marshall.

I'd love to, I've never heard it.

MARSHALL: "No, I do not think we should have gone into Berlin at that time. However, it must be remembered that all this time we were trying to do business with Russia. We'd been fighting with them. They were part of the armed forces, a very decided part. They had played a great part in the fighting—the wearing down of the German strength. And we had to take that into careful regard.

"At that time, toward the close of the struggle, they were exceedingly sensitive . . . looking all the time for something that would indicate that the British and Americans were preparing to go off alone and to settle the thing in a way to their British and American satisfaction and to the disadvantage of the Russians.

"So we were very careful about this. But we were trying very hard to find that basis of negotiation to go along with the Russian government. Eisenhower was in a particularly trying position because, in command of the troops, he was put into constant situations that had to be handled with great delicacy. And almost invariably he had to handle them in a way that displeased one party or the other. And I thought he did extraordinarily well in this matter.

"I must say that all this is very much of a Monday-morning quarterback business because all sorts of things have happened since those days; and our relations with Russia at that time were quite different. They were always delicate. They were always jealous, and it was very, very hard to preserve a coordinated association with them. But we did it to a very large extent at that time, which is unthinkable today in the knowledge of later events. Nobody but the Lord could foresee all that has happened since."

That sounds like the last word, doesn't it, General?

Well, it certainly tells the convictions of a very splendid man, a very fine brain, and certainly a selfless soldier. And I agree with what he had to say.

58

"Monday-morning quarterbacking." As he listens to General
Marshall's recorded voice, Eisenhower reacts with surprise to
the repetition of the phrase he himself used about the Berlin
controversy.

*I think it was Alanbrooke, in fact I know it was, when
somebody asked him what was Churchill's great military virtue, who rather cruelly said, "No grasp of logistics." Somebody else said his strategical grasp was the
great thing.*

59

*General, aside from the inspiration that he was able
to bring to the ordinary soldier, and especially to the
ordinary people of Britain, which was immeasurable,
what would you say was his great contribution to the
military victory?*

His dedication and concentration to the task. And
his ability to communicate his conception to people not
only of your country but of ours. In doing this he won
the loyalty of the American soldiers and of the ordinary
American citizen, almost as much as he did at home.
He was a real unifying influence all the way through. I
cannot tell you how much I owe to him because of what
he did to help cement this kind of feeling right in our
military headquarters. I think that to make any state-
ment derogatory or even commendatory about some
tactical or logistic concept . . . well, he was bigger
than that, more than that.

There was really something in his saying, "Never,
never, never, never give in." The man's bulldog deter-
mination just stood out all over him. And I think that
he's bound to be one of the great men of this whole
century. There's no question about it. And remembered
as that. His name will cover a lot of pages in history
in the future.

*You know the single-phrase dedications that he used
for the volumes of his World War II history: The first,
I think, is "In war, resolution"; and the second is "In
defeat, defiance"; "In victory, magnanimity"; and "In
peace, goodwill." The one that strikes me most is the
phrase "magnanimity." And what I'm thinking of is
this: somewhere, I think in his book on the First World
War, he said, "The first job of a victor is to redress the
wounds of the vanquished." Now, you must have col-
lided with the group—there was a group pretty soon*

Never, never, never, never give in.

61

after the war, right after the victory—that had ideas about what should happen to Germany. Did you talk about that with him?

It became public knowledge really as soon as this crowd sensed the victory. As a matter of fact, just about the time of D-Day, this first came to my attention. A group wanted to destroy the German mark. They wanted to flood the Ruhr mines and in every way possible reduce them to an agricultural economy—just so they had to live there and so they couldn't make war any more.

Did you ever take this up with Churchill?

Oh, yes. He heard about it and he talked about it. And he said, "This is absolutely ridiculous, to think that this great, virile people are going to be denied any progress, any peaceful progress in this world; this is silly, and people who talk this way just don't know human nature." And he was very determined that Germany would be allowed to make its own living and to have a proper place in the world. But he just wanted to make sure that they were so educated, and had learned their lesson so well, that they would no longer be aggressors against a peaceful world, that's all.

General, an incident occurs to me from the First World War that illustrated something that people complained about later. You know Churchill said nobody ever invented the tank, but that he ordered the first set. He didn't call them tanks. He called them land-ships, in March 1915. And he ordered, I think, eighteen land-ships. He did this as First Lord of the Admiralty. He asked no permission of anybody. He didn't ask the War Cabinet. He had no appropriation. And it was a sort of scandal later—except that the tank worked.

62

World War I land-ships.

Now, what occurs to me is, there was a tremendous blowup among the soldiers, the generals, when he introduced the tank. Did he ever try, that you can remember, to—in a mischievous way or a serious way— circumvent your military authority?

No, never. As a matter of fact, of course, he was dealing here with an Allied Commander and he played the game right down the line. We had some very serious arguments, but we did so on the most friendly basis. Never did I see the slightest hint of his trying to go around my authority or doing anything behind my back.

You think then, General, that the vendettas and the resentments which have been spewed out in so many of the memoirs were atypical?

That is correct. As a matter of fact, the worst thing that anybody can do, in my opinion, is to keep an exact diary, because then he will put down every little resentment he had against Bill Smith or Joe Doakes. He will note everything that annoys him. Finally, his editors get hold of this and they say, "Oh, this is a gold mine." They take the things that he said and even emphasize them—the frictional type of entry—instead of those things which show that he thought things were going pretty well. I despise daily biographies as showing real history. I don't believe they do.

But there must have been times when your subordinates burst out with a little chauvinistic zeal: "Damn the British, or damn the Americans." Did you have a rule about that, General?

Yes, I did, in my own headquarters. Any time that I saw a man condemning somebody else and saying that he was a British so-and-so or an American so-and-so, I just said there was an order: he would be relieved.

Now the only man I relieved was in Africa, a man who damned some *confrère,* and he used the adjective, "He was a British so-and-so." And I said, "Well, now, look, if you didn't like the guy and you differed with him I don't care how harshly you argued, but you said this: that he was a *British* so-and-so. Go home." And he did go home.

And he was actually relieved?

Sent home. I tell you the strength of a coalition, whether it's NATO or the two of us in World War II, is the good faith of everybody else . . . the fact that you're trying to forget nationality, objectively approach a problem and say how do we solve this as soldiers or sailors or as airmen, how do we win this victory? What can we do? Or, how can we save ourselves until something else can be done? And I'll tell you that Mr. Churchill was almost the ideal man for observing the spirit of the coalition.

Churchill said he was half-American and wholly British. As you know, his American parent was the beautiful Jennie Jerome of Brooklyn. In fact, he mentioned this double heritage in an address before a special session of the United States Congress. He said:

> *"I cannot help reflecting that if my father had been American and my mother British, instead of the other way round, I might have got here on my own."*

You know that Churchill was a proud member of the order of Cincinnatus, which is restricted to direct decendants of the field officers of General Washington's army.

General, I see from your painting of Churchill above the mantelpiece that there's one avocation you shared with the great man.

FOLLOWING PAGES Churchill addressing Congress in 1941. "If my father had been American and my mother British, I might have got here on my own."

I like to try to paint. I know nothing about it, never had a lesson. But it really is a fascinating thing to do. And of course, I tried portraits. Right after Churchill died, I saw this portrait of him, I believe, in a magazine. And I got hold of it and I tried all winter to get it, to make it the way I wanted it. I didn't quite succeed in doing it the way I wanted, but it's as good as I can do.

Did he ever do a portrait of you?

No, I don't think he ever painted portraits. But I'll try anything.

He put you on to painting, is that it?

Yes. He liked it, and he recommended it to me. I
started really in 1948. I'll tell you an opinion of his
work. Sir Oswald Birley once painted a portrait of me;
and we talked a great deal. He was a famous painter
in England. And he said to me that if Mr. Churchill
had given as much attention to painting as he did to
politics that he would have been the greatest painter of
the modern world. That's a great tribute, I think.

Of course, we might have lost the war!

Well, that would have been a very disagreeable alternative to making him the greatest painter.

By the way, General, this is a frivolous note. But it is a note that's never been written, so far as I've seen. I noticed when Churchill was stomping over the ruins of the London bombings and when he was out in France with the troops, he was always smoking a long cigar. I never saw Churchill smoke half a cigar.

To my mind, I never saw him with less than a half of those big cigars smoked. Now I've seen him lay one down on the edge of a car floor as he got out, and come back to pick it up, take a look at it, throw it away. Light another one, and another half-inch would be gone. He just—he seemed to like to light the cigars. Of course, he never put the cigar in his mouth when he lighted it. He would take and hold the match until the cigar was lighted, and then he'd puff through the whole cigar. And those big, big expensive cigars, he just loved them. He might light a cigar three or four times, but he seldom got more than a little of it smoked.

We often get the idea, from books, of Churchill as a bubbling, always-triumphant war leader. I wonder if in your experience, General, you ever saw him in despair? What I have in mind particularly is when he sent the Prince of Wales *and* Repulse *to Singapore, which he thought would be a great symbol of naval power, and two weeks later they were at the bottom of the ocean.*

Churchill and his famous cigar.

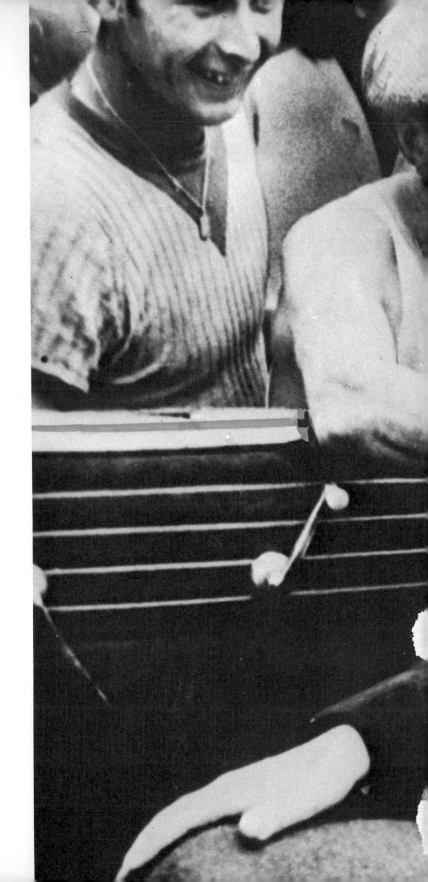

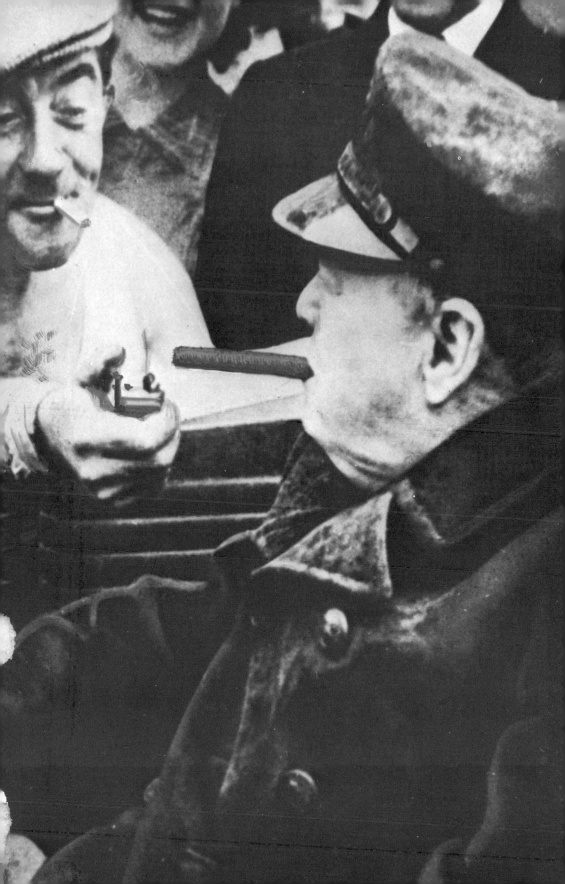

A friend of his said he came into the room that night when he'd heard the news and Churchill said, "A thousand fine men, gone," and he put his head in his hands. In your experience did you ever see any despair, moments of despair?

I saw him shortly after that in late December in Washington when he came over with his own Chiefs of Staff. And he mentioned that then. But he'd gotten over the shock.

I saw him in a possibly similar situation when we lost Tobruk in June 1942. Tobruk had become sort of a symbol of British defiance and a refusal to be defeated in the desert. No matter how those campaigns flowed east and west, Tobruk held. And here suddenly, with no reason that anyone could see, a great many men surrendered the whole city. And I thought he showed very great disappointment, there's no question.

The man was determined never to show a defeated face to anyone publicly, certainly. And he quickly recovered. But there was no question it hurt him deeply.

Of course you know, General, he was very much criticized especially in Parliament—not for showing the face of despair, but for not seeming to recognize the actual criticism that was made of him about the conduct of the war. And at one point somebody said if he'd only look into the surveys of public opinion, he wouldn't be quite so cheerful and heroic all the time.

FOLLOWING PAGES Churchill acknowledges cheers of the crew H.M.S. *Prince of Wales*. Later, when the battleship was sunk, he said in despair, "A thousand fine men, gone."

75

Churchill was criticized for not keeping his ear to the ground.

He said, "I read in the papers that leaders should keep their ear to the ground. I don't think the British nation would look up to a leader who was detected in that somewhat ungainly posture."

Well, he was exactly right . . . did you ever hear the story of the *Bismarck?* I forget the British Admiral's name. He told the story himself. He wirelessed Churchill. "The *Bismarck* is a wreck. The crew has left her but she won't sink. And I've got just enough oil in my ship to get home." The Prime Minister sent him a cable, "You stay there until the *Bismarck* is on the bottom; and we'll send out and tow you in."

A victory to him wasn't a victory—just like Nelson—until the last ship was down on the ocean, that's all. He was a very determined man.

And from away back he reveled in the military life. I remember that in 19 . . . I think it was '35, when Churchill was out of power and out of favor, in what he called the years of the locust, he came to the United

78

States. He spent three weeks walking over the battle-fields of Stonewall Jackson. When he came to Washington he had dinner in the Senate with Senators Robinson, Borah, and Vandenberg and he bored them stiff with talk about Stonewall Jackson. At the end of the dinner as he left, Senator Borah said to Vandenberg, "Senator, there's a man like Cicero who is going to moon his life away thinking what a great general he could have been."

I never heard that story. But I knew he had once said to General Harold Alexander, who, by the way, was a dashing-looking officer, "Yours is the life I would most like to live." I always thought that General Alexander was Churchill's favorite general, personally. Alexander was a considerate man—a gentleman. He was always ready to make allowances for the other fellow's foibles and conceptions. And so while he'd never allow a step to be made he thought would be a mistake, there was no harshness in his character. Every American who served under Alexander thought the world of him—and a lot of them did, a lot of them

We'll fight on the beaches, on the sea, and in the air.

served on his staff. I always kept my high admiration and affection for Alexander.

I've often wondered, General, how many people on both sides of the Atlantic who were moved by Churchill's eloquence, especially when England stood alone in 1940, realized what a very close call it was. Even Churchill's enemies said he made the great speech at the right time. Among the broadcasts forever to be remembered:

> *"We'll fight on the beaches, on the sea, and in the air— until we rid the earth of his shadow."*

Didn't he even say, "If necessary we will hit them on the head with beer bottles?"

At the end of the broadcast, he turned to whoever was standing by the microphone and he put his hand over it and he said, "And we will fight them with beer bottles, because that's about all we have to work with."

General, when the war was over the point was made that your job was to destroy Hitler. That had been your brief. It was done. Hitler was beaten. Now I've often wondered if you saw Churchill immediately after the election of 1945. Because at that time, he wrote the bitterest sentence that he ever wrote in his life: "Thus then, on the night of the tenth of May at the outset of this mighty battle, I acquired the chief power in the State, which henceforth I wielded in ever-growing measure for five years three months of world war, at the end of which time, all our enemies having unconditionally surrendered or being about to do so, I was immediately dismissed by the British electorate from all further conduct of their affairs."

Yes. I tell you what happened. As a matter of fact, something that touched me deeply. I had just heard the news. I was, of course, shocked. And I got a message from Churchill. The message was this: "General, I'd like to take a rest in the south of France." That was an area I controlled. He said, "Could you put me up in one of your villas?"

Now, only a couple of days before, I had writtten an order, and I said all the villas we had down there (for the tired soldiers and officers) should be turned back to the French. Luckily they hadn't operated too quickly; and we still had the villa that I had occupied a couple of times, for about twenty-four hours, down near Cannes. And I sent a message to my old friend, I said, "I can put you up, I can put you up beautifully."

I sent down to him a case of the champagne that I knew he always drank, and a few other presents of that kind and stored them in the house; and said, there they are. We made it so that he had no worries at all; and he spent the time painting. He came to see me before he went out, and he just had a wonderful time.

General, when Churchill died there was an official American delegation, as I recall, headed by the Chief Justice, appointed by the President, who was sick at the time. But I think I'm right in saying you were the only American citizen who was invited by the British, and by the family, to come over and say something. And it's often struck me that this must have been a very satisfying moment in your life; that you were now retired from all official life and that you went over as a private citizen.

I was a bit frightened. But highly complimented. I was very proud that the British people, the family and government wanted me to do something because they knew, certainly, of my affection and my loyalty. Because of that, I resolved that what I would say on this occasion would be of my own composition.

The following are General Eisenhower's words, spoken in London on January 30, 1965, as the Churchill cortege moved through the sorrowing streets and as the barge carrying his coffin up the Thames faded in the mist.

Upon the mighty Thames, a great avenue of history, move at this moment to their final resting place the mortal remains of Sir Winston Churchill. He was a great maker of history, but his work done, the record closed, we can almost hear him, with the poet, say:

Sunset and evening star,
And one clear call for me!

. . . .

twilight and evening bell
and after that the dark!
And may there be no sadness of farewell,
When I embark.

84

As I, like all other free men, pause to pay a personal tribute to the giant who now passes from among us, I have no charter to speak for my countrymen— only for myself. But, if in memory, we journey back two decades to the time when America and Britain stood shoulder to shoulder in global conflict against tyranny, then I can presume—with propriety, I think —to act as spokesman for the millions of Americans who served with me and their British comrades during three years of war in this sector of the earth.

To those men Winston Churchill *was* Britain—he was the embodiment of British defiance to threat, her courage in adversity, her calmness in danger, her moderation in success. Among the Allies his name was spoken with respect, admiration, and affection. Although they loved to chuckle at his foibles, they knew he was a staunch friend. They felt his inspirational leadership. They counted him a fighter in their ranks.

The loyalty that the fighting forces of many nations here serving gave to him during that war was no less strong, no less freely given, than he had, in such full measure, from his own countrymen.

An American, I was one of those Allies. During those dramatic months, I was privileged to meet, to talk, to plan, and to work with him for common goals.

Out of that association an abiding—and to me precious—friendship was forged; it withstood the trials and frictions inescapable among men of strong convictions, living in the atmosphere of war.

The war ended, our friendship flowered in the later and more subtle tests imposed by international politics. Then, each of us, holding high official posts in his own nation, strove together so to concert the strength of our two peoples that liberty might be preserved among men and the security of the free world wholly sustained.

Through a career during which personal victories alternated with defeats, glittering praise with bitter criticism, intense public activity with periods of semi-retirement, Winston Churchill lived out his fourscore and ten years.

With no thought of the length of the time he might be permitted on earth, he was concerned only with the quality of the service he could render to his nation and to humanity. Though he had no fear of death, he coveted always the opportunity to continue that service.

At this moment, as our hearts stand at attention, we say our affectionate, though sad, goodbye to the leader to whom the entire body of free men owes so much.

In the coming years, many in countless words will strive to interpret the motives, describe the accomplishments, and extol the virtues of Winston Churchill —soldier, statesman, and citizen that two great countries were proud to claim as their own. Among all the things so written or spoken, there will ring out through all the centuries one incontestable refrain: Here was a champion of freedom.

May God grant that we—and the generations who will remember him—heed the lessons he taught us: in his deeds, in his words, in his life.

May we carry on his work until no nation lies in captivity; no man is denied opportunity for fulfillment.

And now, to you Sir Winston—my old friend—farewell!

Westminster Abbey. "Churchill *was* Britain."

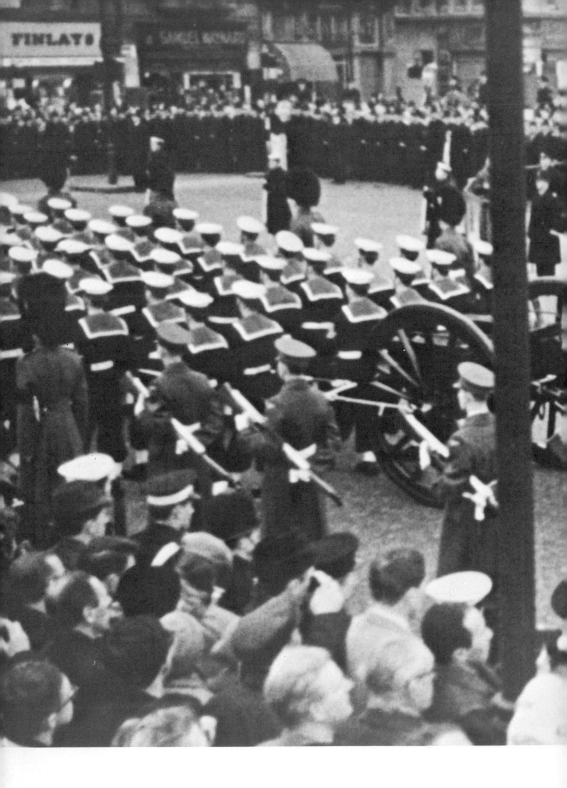

Crowds watch as the caisson proceeds slowly through the streets of London.

St. Paul's Cathedral. As the Prime Minister had requested, the choir sang "The Battle Hymn of the Republic," written by an American, Julia Ward Howe: "He has sounded forth the trumpet that shall never call retreat."

The coffin on the way to its journey up the Thames.

River derricks dipped in unison as the funeral barge passed.

And now, to you, Sir Winston—my old friend—farewell.

Acknowledgments

The editor expresses his thanks to the Dwight D. Eisenhower Estate and to the ABC-TV network for their kind cooperation. In addition, grateful acknowledgment is made to the following individuals for their assistance: to Richard Hanser, historian; to Guy Fraumeni for permission to reproduce his maps; and to Sam Berman for his cartoon of Winston Churchill. For photographic production, thanks are due to Daniel W. Jones, Helen Buttfield, Edward Cullen, and Sol Kasdan; and, for photographic research, to Janet Berger (England) and Barbara Monks (United States). Excerpts from General Marshall's taped report explaining why the Allies did not take Berlin are reprinted with permission of the George C. Marshall Foundation and The Viking Press, publisher of two biographies of Marshall by Forrest C. Pogue, *The Education of A General* (1963) and *Ordeal and Hope* (1966).

Photographic credits: Associated British Pathé, Ltd., 84, 87, 88–89, 90–91, 92–93, 94, 95. Dwight D. Eisenhower Library, title page. Fox Photos, Ltd., 39. Hearst Metrotone News, 50–51. The Imperial War Museum, 34–35, 36–37, 47, 63, 76–77, 80, 81. James Nelson Productions, Inc., 9, 16, 19, 48–49, 59, 68, 69, 79. Thomsen Newspapers Picture Service (Topix), 29. United Press International, Inc., 57, 66–67, 72–73. U.S. Army, 25. U.S. Army Signal Corps, 44–45. Wide World Photos, 20, 24, 53, 61, 70, 74.